First published 1999
• Text Copyright © Julie Statham
Copyright photos © Julie Statham, Len Port, Joan Gay, Peter Daughtrey.

Published by Peter Daughtrey and Len Port
(Vista Ibérica Publicações)
• N.I.P.C. 900398086
Urbanização Lagoa - Sol • Lote 1 - B • 8400 Lagoa
Tel: (082) 340660 • Fax: (082) 343088
ISBN 972-8044-25-9 • *Depósito Legal Nº 140̲*
Printing: Empresa Litográfica do Sul S̲

Every reasonable care has been take̲ ̲ ̲ ̲ ̲ng the information
in this book, but no responsibility ca̲ ̲ ̲ ̲ y ̲ne author or publisher for any
misunderstandings, problems or claims arising from any errors.

D1436104

THE WALKS

A circular walk around the small nature reserve of Esteveira, a sand dune sanctuary on the west coast. For lovers of plants, it is a 'must'.

A walk along the Atlantic coast west of Aljezur where the sand dune system lies on top of 50-metre high cliffs. Many rare plants grow here.

The path between the villages of Salema and Luz is a great walk because it includes some of the best coastal views in the Algarve.

The country-folk you will encounter along the way on this lovely walk north of Lagos still follow an age-old, traditional way of life.

This large man-made lake in the heart of rolling countryside near Lagos provides a perfect setting for peaceful walking.

The Walks

THE WALKS

THE WALKS

INTRODUCTION

The Algarve is an ideal place to walk. This region had never been associated with walking until recently, but an increasing number of visitors are now beginning to realise that there is far more to the Algarve than just its famous coastline. The scenery here is superb wherever you go. There are the most wonderful views, enhanced by a quality of light that is sharp and clear. There are villages that appear to belong to a bygone age, remote areas where the donkey is still the most used form of transport and ancient monuments lie waiting to be discovered.

To find the 'real' Algarve you must park your car and explore on foot. The beauty of this region is that within minutes of leaving the main road you can find yourself completely alone, amid a deafening silence broken only by birdsong, where the fragrance of the wild flowers and herbs can fill up your senses and the panorama of unspoilt countryside is a feast for the eyes.

There is no designated network of footpaths here and, because the number of footpaths and tracks are countless, people are reluctant to wander far. This is understandable. The walks in this book have been designed to allow you to get out and explore the countryside with confidence. They offer a wide variety of scenery: along coastal paths, down mountain passes, through river valleys and over rolling hillsides. There are walks for everyone.

WALKING IN THE ALGARVE

WALK GRADES AND TIMES

The walks in this book have been designed to be enjoyed. They are, therefore, not particularly strenuous or difficult and usually follow well-trodden tracks and paths. Those few walks that have been classified 'moderately difficult' involve either an ascent or descent of some kind, which will get the heart pumping but not for long. These are not walks for serious hikers, but more for those who like to gently roam.

I am not a fast walker. I like to appreciate the countryside through which I am walking: I like to chat with my friends and when going uphill I often stop and have a 'breather'. You may be able to complete the walks much faster than I have done; the times are only there for guidance. Many people like to know how far they have walked. I do too, but it is very difficult to be accurate when measuring distances. My average walking speed is 4km an hour.

ACCESS

Provided you do not deliberately cross fences designed to keep people and animals out, or damage crops and vegetation, there is no great concern about trespass. It is rare to see 'privado' notices except next to new villas owned by foreigners. Local people are generally welcoming and friendly. It is very apparent that most

Introduction

Algarvians do not enjoy a wealthy lifestyle, so as a courtesy to them, if you take your dog on a walk, make sure it is under control at all times.

Whereas fences are rare in the Algarve, dry-stone walls in some areas are very common. These have not been built to keep people out, but are the result of the land being cleared for cultivation. It is also common to see boundary markers - small stone posts or piles of white painted stones - while walking. These do not indicate footpaths as in some countries; they are land boundaries.

HUNTING

Hunting is still very popular here in the Algarve as can be witnessed from the number of gun cartridges on the ground in hunting zones. The main targets for the hunters are rabbits, foxes, hares, wild boar and all kinds and sizes of birds.

During the 'open' season, hunting is restricted to Sunday, Thursday and public holidays. Please do avoid walking on these days unless you are very sure that hunting is not permitted in the area where you want to walk. Personal experience of walking in the wrong place at the wrong time, and having to dive into the bushes as shots whistled past my ears, is something I do not want to repeat.

DOGS

Any visitor to the Algarve will soon realise that there are many dogs around and they can be very noisy. Most dogs are kept outdoors and will let their owner know of your presence long before you know of theirs. Although they can sound extremely fierce, they are very rarely vicious. If you are unsure, the best precaution is to bend down, pick up a stone and threaten to throw: the dog will back off. If no stones are available, then an imaginary stone can be just as effective!

THE RIGHT GEAR

Correct footwear is very important. Do not attempt any of the

walks in heels, flip-flops or slingbacks. These will not give you enough support. Regular outdoor shoes, walking boots and trainers will.

Clothing is a matter of personal choice. I would suggest taking a small backpack or bag with you on the longer walks. Pack a lightweight sweater or waterproof to protect against the winds which can blow up, especially in the afternoon, or the odd unexpected shower.

Always carry some water. This is very important in summer. So is protection from the sun. Apply sunscreen and wear a hat. It is amazing how hungry you can get when out walking, so take a piece of fruit or a light snack with you. Many of the walks have great places to picnic.

Although the Algarve has more sunshine hours than anywhere else in Europe, it does sometimes rain, and when it rains, it tends to rain all day. If you go walking after a lot of rain, many of the paths will be muddy and sometimes slippery. In these conditions, the right footwear is even more important.

CAR THEFTS

The crime rate is low here in the Algarve, but there are always those who are tempted by an empty car. Always take your passport and valuables with you.

ALGARVE SCENERY

There is so much beauty here. It is not a brash beauty, but one that is altogether more subtle and alluring. You cannot take this landscape for granted, because it is so varied with a different picture to be seen around every corner. Trying to understand the variety is difficult as the geology is complex, but in broad terms the region can be divided into three zones: the *serras* (hills), the central 'Barrocal' and the Littoral or coastal strip.

To the north and west, the Serra de Monchique is a distinctive area of igneous rocks, rising to a peak at Foia (902m), the highest point in the Algarve. The soils are fertile and there is plenty of water available, mainly from underground springs, allowing the local population to intensively cultivate the terraced slopes.

Shales underlie the remainder of the *serras*. Deep valleys separated by high ridges are characteristic of the landscape and on the west coast the shales form tall, dark cliffs. Soils are poor and acidic. The whole area was once covered in forests of cork

and holm oak, but these were removed during the 15th century when wood was needed to build sailing ships for the Portuguese voyages of discovery. Winter rains then washed the topsoil away and led to erosion of the land. In an attempt to grow more wheat during the First World War, those trees that had grown up were cut down again and once more the shallow top soil was washed away. Today, the high serras are covered in forests of eucalyptus, pine, cork and holm oak, but on the lower reaches the vegetation is much more scrub-like. Here the cistus bush dominates, especially the large, green, sticky-leaved variety with its distinctive white flowers. Lavender, heather and the cork oak are also to be found.

The 'Barrocal' is the name given to a variety of limestone hills that extend from Cape St. Vincent in the west, almost through to the Spanish border. The whole area is roughly elliptical in shape, with its widest part in the central Algarve. In the west, these limestones end at Cape St. Vincent with massive cliffs more than 80m high, but between there and Lagos, the coastline is more undulating. The chemical composition of the limestones is extremely varied. The purest have been used for centuries to make quicklime for whitewashing houses. The remains of old kilns can be found dotted around the countryside.

This is a highly productive area where thousands of almond trees grow together with fig, olive, carob and many other crops. Where there is less cultivation, the plant life is very characteristic of limestone areas: dwarf palms, mastic and turpentine bushes, lavender, holly oak with its prickly leaves, wild jasmine and the small flowered cistus can always be seen both inland and along the coast. In spring this whole region is home to a profusion of wild flowers, including tiny narcissi, tulips, jonquils and irises, which grow among the rocks and boulders. Many varieties of orchids, especially the bee and mirror orchids, are also to be found in the less disturbed spots.

Most of the southern Algarve coastline is made up of relatively young, iron-rich sediments. It is the variable iron content that gives the famous Algarve cliffs their bright, orange colours. Because the sediments are young, they are also 'soft' and have been eroded by the sea and the wind into an amazing variety of forms, including rock arches, stacks and caves.

Within these sediments there are pockets of even younger sands dating from the Ice Age. The dunes found along the clifftops are derived from them, as are the large-scale sandbanks seen at the mouths of the rivers and along the coast east of Faro. Here there is an extensive system of sand spits, island and banks behind which salt marshes have developed, giving rise to a unique flora and fauna. This area is now recognised as one of Europe's most important wetland sites and was designated the Ria Formosa Nature Park in 1988.

BACK TO NATURE

A circular walk around the small nature reserve of Esteveira

Walk time: an easy 1hr 15mins; distance 2.5km.
Walk grade: very easy; one for all the family.

The small nature reserve of Esteveira is a real gem. There are no signs to it and so it appears to have few visitors, like so much of this Atlantic coastline. It is a dune area and the habitat is very fragile, so please stay on the existing paths. For lovers of plants, this walk is a 'must' and you can easily spend two or three hours here. Common plants to be found include the hottentot fig, sage-leaved cistus, Portuguese milk vetch, wild antirrhinums, thrift, thyme and red oxalis.

START OF THE WALK

Drive north from Aljezur to the village of Rogil. At the far end of the village, turn left at the Esteveira signpost. Continue until this road runs out after about 10km. Park the car.

THE WALK

Walk along the track to your left. It passes between two houses. Soon after you will notice a deep ravine on your right. When the now sandy track heads downwards, the side marked by a wooden fence, take a small sandy path off to your left. It climbs to the top of the cliff.

There are numerous paths which cross this reserve and you are free to explore. However, to see all the reserve, keep to the path which runs parallel to the cliff edge. This soon brings you to a flat shelf where you have wonderful views along the coast northwards. On a clear day you can see as far as Sines.

Follow the path around to your left and soon you come to another shelf, this time with views southwards and equally as good.

The path continues to run parallel to the cliff edge until it meets a small, wet area where giant reeds can be seen. The path then skirts directly behind them. Eventually it reaches the edge of a second ravine, which marks the southern extent of the reserve, before heading inland. Soon the path winds its way between pine trees to the left and cultivated fields to the right. Keep on this path and it will eventually bring you back to the two houses seen at the beginning of the walk. At the track, turn right and you should see your car ahead of you.

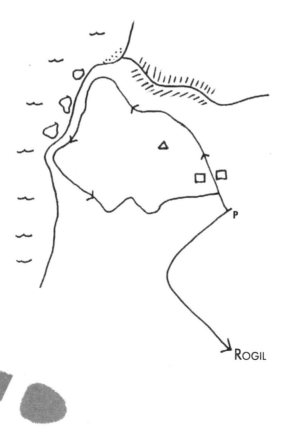

IS THIS REALLY THE ALGARVE?

A walk along the Atlantic coast west of Aljezur.

Walk time: Allow 2 hours 30 minutes to complete the whole walk. Total distance 7km.

Walk grade: Relatively easy. Some parts of the paths pass through dunes which are very sandy and are quite heavy going on the legs, but don't let this put you off.

This coastal walk is along the cliffs from the small village of Espartal to Ponta da Atalaia. Much of the area has been shaped by an extensive sand dune system that lies on top of 50-metre high cliffs. The whole area is itself a unique habitat for many rare plants and is now a protected landscape within the Sudoeste Alentejano e Costa Vincentina Natural Park.

Endemic plants that can be found in the dunes include thyme, wild antirrhinums, thrift, yellow restharrow and orchids. Even if you are not a real plant-lover, this is still a walk to be enjoyed. There are great views, with amazingly contorted cliffs and the sea breaking over offshore rocks of all shapes and sizes.

START OF THE WALK

Just before entering Aljezur from the south there is a turning on the left to Espartal. At the top of the hill turn right, again following the sign to Espartal. This is a new road system and makes for easy driving, allowing you to appreciate views down the valley of Aljezur. Old salt pans can be seen close to the mouth of the river. The road descends into Espartal before climbing again. Just after leaving the village you will see a small picnic area on your right. Immediately after this there is rough track on your right. Turn here and drive towards the clifftop. Park your car just as the track bears round to the left.

THE WALK

Before setting off, walk to the edge of the cliff where you have fine views northwards along the coast. Proceed up the rough track. You may see cars and vans owned by local fishermen parked along the way, but do not be tempted to drive. You cannot properly appreciate the scenery from a car window!

When the track ends at a small turning circle, you will notice a sandy path off to your left. This is your path, but there are many other pathways winding through the vegetation, some less sandy than others. Your goal is the headland in front of you with a distinct offshore rock outcrop. Just follow the trails. At one point they do go slightly inland to avoid a small gully. You cannot go wrong if you remember to keep the sea on your right-hand side. There are several small, wet areas marked by reeds. These should not present any problem, although they may be muddy so watch your feet.

When you have reached Ponta da Atalaia or have just had enough, turn around and follow the same path back. It's easy!

CLIFFTOPS AND BEACHES

The coastal path from Salema to Luz

Walk time: Salema to Luz, a comfortable 3 hours, total distance 10Kms. Salema to Burgau, allow 1 hour 45 minutes. Burgau to Luz, allow 1 hour 15 minutes.

Walk grade: moderately easy. Some of the paths are quite stony and there are several fairly steep climbs between Salema and Burgau. The path between Burgau and Luz is much easier and relatively flat.

Coastal paths are always popular. I believe it has much to do with that timeless attraction - the sea. If at the same time you have wonderful scenery and good weather, then you have all the ingredients for a perfect walk. This is one of those great walks, but only try all or part of it when the weather is fine with good visibility, because the coastal views are some of the best in the Algarve and it would be a shame to miss them.

The walk starts at the fishing village of Salema. This is a real fishing village and every day the locals queue to buy fish straight from the boats as they arrive back from working along the coastline. The walk passes over the cliffs to drop down at the ancient site of Boca do Rio before climbing up and over to the beautiful beach of Cabanhas Velhas. From here the path ascends and descends before reaching another fishing village, Burgau. After Burgau, the scenery changes and everything becomes much flatter as you follow the path to the holiday village of Luz.

START OF THE WALK

Take the EN125 south from Lagos. After about 15km you pass the village of Budens, the road climbing up to some traffic lights with the Parque da Floresta Golf and Leisure complex on your right. Turn left at the lights and almost immediately left again. This road leads you into the centre of Salema where you should be able to park your car. Alternatively, you could take a taxi (they are relatively inexpensive) or catch the bus from Lagos or Luz.

SALEMA TO BURGAU

Looking towards the sea in Salema, take Rua dos Pescadores, the small street off to your left close to the telephone boxes. This is a pretty, typical Portuguese street that has not yet been spoilt by tourist development. It climbs to the top of the village where it opens out on to a much wider but unsurfaced road. Keep straight ahead. To your left, there is a small valley covered with fig and almond trees, which almost certainly have seen more productive days.

The road eventually rises to meet another road to your left, but just before this on your right there is a small path that climbs steeply uphill. Yes, you must turn here, but fortunately the climb is short! At the top, keep on the track heading toward the sea and soon you will have great views along the coast in both directions. On the cliff top to your left you can see the ruins of a Spanish fort and, below, the small beach of Boca do Rio.

The path forks as it descends. The choice is yours although the right-hand track will give you better views of the coast south towards Salema and beyond.

You now meet an unsurfaced road. If you prefer, you can follow this round to Boca do Rio, or you can take the small track which follows the cliff top. There is a fenced off area to your right which is now in a poor state of repair. It is believed that there are the remains of a Roman settlement here and, indeed, on the cliffs close to the beach you can see the remains of a Roman villa. The fence is supposed to protect the site. Sadly, it is not very effective.

When you reach the beach, proceed to the left and behind the beach bar. You will notice a small river in front of you and to your left you should see a small concrete bridge. Cross the river and turn right to follow the track below the cliffs. Soon you will notice a ruined farmhouse to your left and in front of it a stony track that leads up the hillside. This path, although fairly steep, is the best one to take to the top. There are alternative tracks off to the right, but they follow a much steeper gradient.

Your path will bring you on to a dirt track. Catch your breath and then turn right along the track, which will bring you to the ruined fort. This is a good resting spot with wonderful views.

Refreshed, take any of the narrow paths to the left of the fort. They all meet at some stage and follow the cliff top. Do take care: there are many small loose stones about. Ahead of you there is a large house and eventually your path brings you down to the back of it. Walk behind and around the house to the garages. You will see a track on your left. Follow this but, again, do watch your footing: it is a wide track but it can be a bit stony as it descends to meet another track.

If you turn right at the bottom of the slope you will come to Cabanhas Velhas beach where there is a beach bar. Our path continues by taking the track opposite. It heads uphill to the right, climbing gradually. Fragrant plants and herbs, such as rosemary, thyme and French lavender, now surround you. In spring this area is awash with wild flowers.

Eventually the path flattens out to provide a natural viewing point with fabulous vistas all the way along the coast to Sagres. The route continues by heading downward to meet another track. Turn left and follow this track through a rock cutting and upwards to the top of the hill. Because of its height, the top of the hill provides a unique panorama and on a clear day you can follow the coastline all the way from Cabo Carvoeiro in the east to Sagres in the south.

Continue along the wide track until it forks. The much wider left branch heads away from the sea. You now take a much narrower path which climbs and descends several times as it follows the cliff profile. The path is now very narrow and stony, so take care. The final descent is very steep and you may prefer to descend through the grass at the side of the path.

At the bottom you meet a surfaced road. Turn right and follow it into Burgau. You come to a junction with a bus shelter on your left, Turn right and take the second narrow road on your right - Rua da Praia. Follow this down to the beach.

BURGAU TO LUZ

At the end of the Rua da Praia, the street opens out just before the beach. Turn left and follow another narrow street lined with whitewashed houses. It eventually bends to the right and climbs uphill. To your left there is an apartment block. At the top of the street you meet an unsurfaced track on your left. This almost immediately forks. Take the right path and keep on this, ignoring any side paths.

The path is now very flat, reflecting the horizontal nature of the underlying rocks; this is clearly seen at the cliff face as you walk along. Because it is flat, this is a very popular path and therefore well trodden, so it should be very easy to follow. If in doubt at any time, just remember to follow the path closest to the cliff edge but, of course, do take care!

Eventually you come to a small hill. The coastal path goes straight up and over but, if you prefer, you can take a small path off to the left which brings you all the way around the hill to meet up with the original path. It now heads over some rocks and the cliffs of Luz can clearly be seen in front of you. Again follow the well-trodden path.

The path passes to the side of a villa to avoid a rocky bay and then heads towards the sea and follows the cliffs before narrowing as it passes around the rocks. Here you will notice piles of small stones to the sides of the path. On your left you will pass three large holes. DO TAKE CARE. These holes are not easily seen and indeed a fig tree is growing out of one!

You are now passing to the left of large slabs of rock, which slope gently towards the sea. When you come to a small building, go to the left and you will meet a wide track. Follow this toward Luz. The track eventually becomes a small surfaced road and this will bring you into the centre of Luz opposite the church where you will find the bus stop and taxi rank.

A BYGONE AGE

A walk in the Serra do Espinhaço de Cão.

Walk time: A comfortable two hours.
Walk grade: An easy walk of about 9.6km on very good tracks and one short stony path.

Only half an hour from the popular holiday town of Lagos the local people still follow a traditional way of life. However, traditions are rapidly being lost as the number of abandoned farmhouses seen on this walk will testify. The route offers a fascinating insight into the old ways, as well as being a super walk through wonderful countryside.

START OF THE WALK

Take the N120 from Lagos towards Aljezur. About 10km north of Bensafrim you come to a small hamlet where there is a left turning to Sagres. Take this road and drive for approximately 3km when you will see a derelict house/barn on your right. Opposite, on your left, is a track. Park here. To make sure you are in the correct place, check that you can see a single-storey farmhouse just down the road on the right.

THE WALK

Walk down the surfaced road past the farmhouse where you can often see cork bark drying in the sun. Continue along this road for about 10 minutes and you will see on the hilltop to your right a long single-storey farmhouse, which is almost derelict. Just after this you come to another small house on your right close to the road and opposite this there is a track.

Turn left down the track. Soon you cross a small stream and then pass up between a small avenue of cork trees. The countryside begins to open up before you pass an abandoned farm up on the hillside to your right. Soon you reach another abandoned homestead, which the track passes in front of.

Notice the large pile of slate on the right as you pass by. This would have been hand-picked from the fields to help improve the soil depth and quality!

The track now climbs gently up between fields. Occasionally the local farmer will be grazing his cattle here and may have it roped off. It is to prevent the cattle from straying, not to prevent you from passing through.

In the fields you will see more derelict buildings, indicating that at one time there must have been a small community here.

At the top of the hill, turn right along a track that soon passes through a pine forest and eucalyptus wood. Soon after you emerge from the trees you will notice, on your left, an electric pylon that is larger than the usual, with a box attached to the side. Just in front of this there is a small track to your left. Turn down this track which soon becomes a single path and follows the hillside around to your right. The path is rather stony, but it is still easy walking and finishes just before a small house where you take the path to your left. It leads to a wide track just below.

Turn left and follow the track around to your right, over a small bridge and up a small hill. At the top of the hill there is a crossroads of tracks. Take the left one. It passes two houses on the left and climbs very gently. There are now wonderful panoramic views as you walk along.

You pass a few more houses before the track levels out to pass between large fields and then enters a large eucalyptus plantation. Soon after leaving the trees you come to a fork in the track. Take the right path. You now pass through open countryside once again and, after a gentle climb, you are treated to more wonderful views.

Eventually you come to a meeting of tracks. Turn left to head downhill. You will see a house at the bottom and another on the hilltop ahead. As you pass the first house, which is abandoned, notice the old bread oven and the well with watering troughs for the animals. Now take the track which heads uphill to the other house. The path passes right in front of this house almost over the doorstep. It is hard to imagine that this house is still inhabited. Continue straight on before heading down hill. At the bottom of the hill you pass over a small stream and you should see the road and your car in front of you.

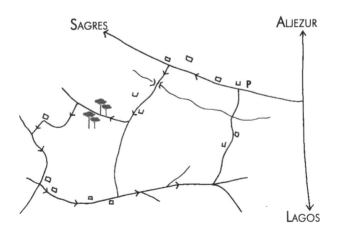

THE BARRAGEM DE BRAVURA

A reservoir in rolling countryside, a perfect setting for walking

Many locals come at the weekend to fish and have a picnic, but during the week it is relatively quiet. It is a great place to relax away from the beaches, and the eucalyptus trees provide welcome shade from the glare of the sun.

START OF THE WALK

If coming from Portimão on the N125, turn right in the centre of Odiáxere into Rua da Barragem. Follow the road through Odiáxere. It is a narrow, surfaced road. Stay on it for 7km when you will get wonderful views over the lake to your left. Continue until the road takes you down to the dam wall, where you can park your car.

LAKESIDE WALK

Walk time: anything from half an hour to two hours.
Walk grade: very easy; level walking on a good track.

Cross the dam and you will see a track on your left running along the side of the lake. This track is easy walking as it follows the water's edge, sometimes leaving it for short instances, but always coming back. Before the track heads uphill and inland, it provides a comfortable hour's walking, so when you feel you have had enough, just turn around and retrace your steps.

LAKESIDE AND COUNTRYSIDE - A CIRCULAR WALK

Walk time: a comfortable three hours.
Walk grade: moderately easy; some of the inland tracks are stony, but never difficult.

Follow the instructions for the lakeside walk. After about an hour of walking the track begins to climb uphill and away from the water. At the top of the hill you meet another track. Turn left and follow the path downhill. You now have superb views over the countryside to the Serra de Monchique and, on a clear day, the telecommunications aerials on the summit of Foia can readily be seen. Continue downhill and you will come to a fork in the track. Our walk follows the right fork, which continues downwards.

However, a detour to the left is to be recommended: after about half a kilometre you will have a great view of another part of this lake and surrounding hillsides. This is a good place for a rest to recharge the batteries before continuing.

Retrace your steps and continue downhill. At the bottom you meet another track. Turn right. The path now follows the hillside as it climbs gently upwards. Ignore any side paths. Eventually, at the top of the climb, you come to a junction of tracks. The one you have been following bears left and passes through a eucalyptus wood. You must take a smaller, much stonier track which heads uphill to your right. At the top of the hill, keep straight on, ignoring paths off to the left and right. As you walk along, you should be able to catch glimpses of the coastline and the town of Lagos on your left between the trees.

Eventually you should see the lake down below on your right side. At the same time, you come across two tracks close together on your right, which head downhill. Ignore both of them!

Soon after, your path too begins to descend, bearing around to the right and following the hillside. On your left there is a steep wooded valley. At the bottom of the slope you meet another track crossing in front of you. Turn right. This track also heads downwards and brings you to a path at the bottom. This is the lakeside track you started out on. Turn left and follow the path back to your car.

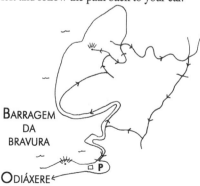

BARRAGEM
DA
BRAVURA

ODIÁXERE

FROM HERE TO ETERNITY

A circular walk high in the Serra de Monchique

Walk time: Allow four hours but you will probably find you can do it in less.

Walk grade: A moderately strenuous walk on good tracks and paths.

Here is a challenging walk that will reward you with the most spectacular views. It begins close to the summit of Foia. The actual summit is best left to the coach loads of holidaymakers, the souvenir shops and the radio telecommunication masts. The views on this walk can easily match those on the summit and in my opinion are even better.

Although this is a great walk it is not suitable for all the family because the path takes you down almost 370 metres into a neighbouring valley and you have to make this up again on the return! The ascent is for the most part gradual, so do not be put off. Your efforts will be not be in vain!

Do take a drink and either a picnic or snack. The walk begins at a height of 800 metres. It can be considerably cooler up there even in the height of summer, so make sure you carry something

warm to wear. It is better to be safe than sorry. Because the views are so spectacular, it is recommended you only try this walk on a clear day.

START OF THE WALK

From Monchique take the road to Foia. Approximately 6km from Monchique you pass a *miradoura* (viewing point) on your left. Soon after this the road bends sharply around to the right and you will notice two tracks off to the left. Take the second one that passes to the right of some abandoned buildings and park the car.

THE WALK

Continue down the track, which passes to the right of the hill ahead. Already there are great views up to the Alentejo off to your right. Soon you come to a fork. Take the left track, which goes gently uphill. Ignore a track off to your left and when you come to another fork, take the right one that goes slightly downhill. You should now see the fire watchtower on the hilltop to your left. This marks the summit of Madrinha, the second highest peak (802m) in the Serra de Monchique.

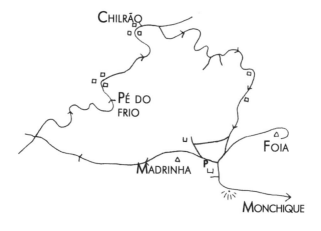

In front, you should be able to make out the west coast and the town of Aljezur. As you continue along, the south coast and the Barragem de Bravura soon come into view. Your track appears to follow a ridge before heading down to a plantation of eucalyptus trees. Ignore any turnings off to left or right; always stay on the main track that leads downwards. When you reach the plantation, the track forks. The choice is yours: you can take either as they meet again further downhill. Both are quite steep with loose stones, so take care.

As you continue descending, you should be able to see another hilltop in front of you with a small building just below the summit. This is Picos (574m). Eventually you meet a wide, unsurfaced road; there is a small white junction box on your right. Turn right on to the road that follows the hillside. This is now very easy walking. You stay on this road for about 4km, passing through the hamlet of Pé do Frio and then Chilrão.

Continue through Chilrão, passing the signpost for Portelo da Viuva. Soon after leaving the village the road bends sharply to the right and you should see a track off to your right which heads uphill. Take this track. Your ascent has now started so just pace yourself. It is mostly gentle and the track underfoot is good. You are rewarded for your efforts with wonderful views towards the Alentejo on your left as you climb. Ignore all paths off to the left and right. Your main track follows the hillside and appears to double back on itself as it heads uphill. You should be able to see the rooftops of derelict houses nestled into the hillside and you are left wondering how people ever lived and survived here. The view just gets better the higher you go.

The track passes just below a derelict building to your left and soon bends sharply left. Ignore a track off to your right which heads downhill. Soon your track swings sharply left again. There is another track off to the right which should also be ignored. Not long after, the terraced slopes of Madrinha and Foia come into view. When this happens, your climb is almost complete!

The track now follows the hillside around and you can see the houses of both Chilrão and Pé do Frio down to your right. As you walk along, you pass several houses that appear derelict and your track takes you through the terracing before you come to a fork. Take the left track which heads uphill to the road and the start of the walk.

Picota

ON TOP OF THE WORLD

A circular walk up to the summit of Picota.

Walk time: This is a comfortable two and a half-hours, but you may want to spend time at the top enjoying the view or having a picnic.

Walk grade: moderately easy. The first part of the walk is uphill, but this is done gradually and the paths and tracks are good. There is a bit of a climb up to the summit, but nothing too difficult and well worth the effort.

Picota is the second highest peak in the Serra de Monchique. It stands across the valley from the highest - Foia - and the town of Monchique lies between the two. Because of the good road to the summit of Foia, it much more popular with visitors, leaving Picota still unspoilt. Just recently the narrow road to the summit has been surfaced, not to accommodate the ever-increasing number of safari jeeps that visit the mountains, but rather to allow better access to the fire watchtower perched on the top.

Picota is still a very quiet and tranquil place and provides wonderful walking in a beautiful setting. When you reach the top the views are quite spectacular and you can easily imagine that you are sitting on top of the world.

START OF THE WALK

Just as you enter the town of Monchique you take a right turn signposted 'Alferce'. Follow the road for about 2kms then look for a small sign on your right to 'Bemposta' and 'Montinhos da Serra'. Turn right. The road goes very steeply uphill for about 1km and then bears right. To your left there is a wide unsurfaced track. Park on the side of the road here.

THE WALK

Head along the unsurfaced track. You will probably notice large blue arrows painted on the bedrock. There are tall eucalyptus trees on either side. When you come to a fork, bear right and almost immediately you will see a turning off to your right. It is quite steep and the track has been covered in concrete. Turn here. Ignore the blue arrows that indicate going straight on. After a very short steepish climb, the concrete runs out and you are back on a wide track that continues to head uphill, then bends right to pass below an old farmstead on your left.

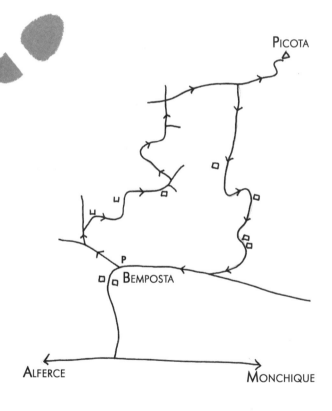

The track is now level and this is a good time to get your breath back and admire the views. Soon the track bends to the left, passing an old house on your left, before turning right and heading towards another house hidden amongst trees to your right. Soon after passing this you will notice a track off to your right. Ignore this. Your track bears left and continues to climb. Not long after, you will see a path off to your left. Turn here leaving the main track. You may spy a red spot painted on the bedrock at the junction of the two paths.

You are now heading upward on a wide path through eucalyptus trees. As you emerge from the trees you have good views to your left. The path now bends sharply to the right around a meadow, the home of tall foxgloves, before passing through eucalyptus trees again. Ignore turnings off to your right and follow the path as it climbs gently to the brow of a hill where you meet a junction of tracks. Turn right.

The path now heads over large exposures of bedrock where you should notice painted orange spots. It is these you now need to follow. The path climbs up a bit more before entering a small wood and becoming single track.

Follow the path with the aid of the spots through the trees. Occasionally you may have to duck to avoid low-growing branches, but soon you will come out onto a small, surfaced road.

Turn left and follow the road. You should soon be able to see the fire watchtower and the trig point that mark the summit of Picota. Just below the summit, the surfaced road ends and you must climb up over the large mass of bedrock. Care is needed as there are a lot of loose stones on the path.

Once you have enjoyed the fabulous views and the satisfied feeling of reaching the top, you must think about returning! Watch your footing on the loose stones. Walking downhill can put considerable strain on your knees, so take it easy. Just follow the surfaced road all the way, ignoring all turnings to left and right. There are wonderful views to be enjoyed across the mountain range north, far into the Alentejo, so do take your time.

Eventually your road emerges from the trees to meet another surfaced road on a bend. Turn right and follow this road for a good 20 minutes, until you come to your car. This part of the walk may sound boring, but it is not. The road follows the side of the hill as it climbs gently upwards passing small homesteads. Each side of the road has been terraced and the land is still worked by hand, producing a large variety of fruit and vegetables. This is a way of life that has almost disappeared in the western world.

THE ALVOR ESTUARY

There are two walks here: the first is a short one around an old salt pan located at the mouth of the river Odiaxere; the second climbs up onto the peninsula before dropping down to the salt marshes of the Alvor estuary.

The rivers Odiaxere and Alvor unite here before flowing into the sea. The whole area is protected by large sandbanks where local fishermen collect clams and other shells at low tide and it is home to a wide variety of birds. The protection from the ravages of the sea has allowed salt marshes to form along both rivers; a small peninsular separates them providing wonderful views over the whole area.

Walk time: Walk one: a comfortable forty minutes, however if you are a birdwatcher you could be here all day.

Walk two: an easy one-hour and three-quarters.

Walk grade: Walk One: Very easy.

Walk Two: Easy, although there is a short steep climb at the beginning, which can be avoided by a short detour.

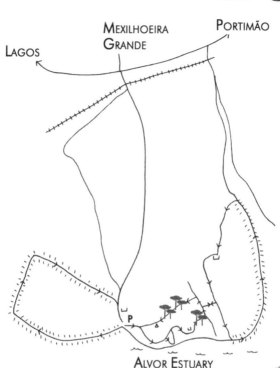

ALVOR ESTUARY

START OF THE WALK:

To reach the estuary by car you must turn off the EN125 at Mexilhoeira Grande. The turning is opposite that for the village itself. It is a narrow lane directly beside a garden centre. You drive down the lane to the very end and park in a clearing close to the waters edge. Alternatively, you can take the train from the direction of either Lagos or Portimão to Mexilhoeira Grande station and walk down the lane, a distance of 2.5km.

THE WALKS
Walk One

Walk to the waters edge and you will see a track off to your right. Follow this all the way and it will bring you back to your car - nothing could be simpler!

Walk Two

To the left of the car park you will see a wide track heading up the hillside. This is your path. If it really is too steep, then walk back along the track you drove on. At the ruined farmhouse, pass behind and walk through the grass up to meet the other track. Now continue straight on to a clearing on your right where you have a great view of the sandbanks and beyond to the town of Lagos. Follow the track for a short distance before turning right on to a narrow path that passes downwards through the bushes.

Once at the bottom of the slope, turn right again and the path will bring you to the water's edge.

Now take a wider path that heads uphill. You should see the

trig point amongst the trees in front of you. Once back at the top, turn right on to a wide track. You again have good views towards Lagos. When the track eventually bears left, you have a wonderful view directly in front of you of the old fishing village of Alvor.

At this point you should see a path leading off to your left that passes in front of an old ruined house before heading towards a small wood of umbrella pines. As you enter the wood, the path becomes very unclear. Don't worry. Continue straight ahead through the trees. The path climbs gently up before emerging from the trees at an overgrown hedge. Turn left and follow the hedge to the end where you will see an old watering tank. Pass behind this and you will see a wide track to your right.

Once on the track, turn left and almost immediately right on to another track that heads downhill where you will see a rather dilapidated wall. Turn right and follow the wall. The path will bring you on to the salt marsh.

Continue straight on and follow the path around the marsh, which is on your left. Ahead is the village of Alvor.

You stay on this path for a good 30 minutes until the small stream and the marsh end. At this point turn left and follow the edge of the marsh to a fence. Turn left again and stay close to the fence as you head towards a small hillock. Once there, walk around the bottom of the hillock and you will see a footpath.

Follow the footpath although at times it may be hard to make out, so just stay close to the fence. This is not difficult walking. Eventually the fence gives way to a field. Stay close to it and at its far end bear left to head towards an abandoned farm. Once there, turn right to pass behind the house and you will meet a track. Turn left and follow the track until you meet another leading off to your right.

Turn here and you now climb gently uphill where you meet another track. Turn right again. Not long after that, turn left on to another path that passes through the trees. Soon you pass behind the trig point. Stay on the track and it will bring you back to your starting point.

BETWEEN TWO RIVERS

The Morgado de Arge

Walk time: Walk one - an easy hour and a half.
Walk two - a comfortable two and a half-hours.

Walk grade: Walk one - easy on very good paths.
Walk two - moderately easy; there are some short steep uphill climbs and some of the paths are stony.

The Morgado de Arge lies between the Arade and Boina rivers, just north of Portimao, and can be seen by all who travel along the EN125 as they cross the new bridge. The walk itself follows the estuary for a while before moving inland and climbing gently upwards, where you will be rewarded with a fabulous panorama.

This is a walk of two halves: for those who like a leisurely stroll you can just walk the first part; for those who prefer a little more 'meat' to their walks, the second half includes a climb up to the local trig point. The variety of plant life seen on this walk is tremendous. The path crosses a limestone knoll on the first half of the walk and here you can see all the lime-loving plants which make the Algarve so special. In spring, orchids can be found. The second part of the walk passes over a small lens of deep red sandstone (the same stone was used to build the castle at Silves). There is a marked change in vegetation, which is short-lived before changing again as the path crosses over to the stony schists with their poor quality soils and home to the ever-present sticky cistus.

THE START OF THE WALK

The Morgado de Arge is just off the main road up to Monchique. About 2km after leaving the EN125 in the direction of Monchique you will cross a fairly narrow bridge. Less than a kilometre after the bridge you will see a collection of fairly derelict buildings on your right behind some trees. Hidden amongst these trees is an unsurfaced road. Turn right onto the road and drive past the buildings, this is the hamlet of Arge. You will notice several small houses on the left. Park by the last one where you will see a track off to the left, some large-scale works to improve the drainage of the area and an old pump house.

THE WALK

Continue up the main unsurfaced road, which you drove along past the drainage works and soon you will come to an abandoned primary school on your left. There is a track off to your right: turn down here. The path passes through abandoned fields and then bears quite sharply right passing in front of a small house, the home of several noisy dogs.

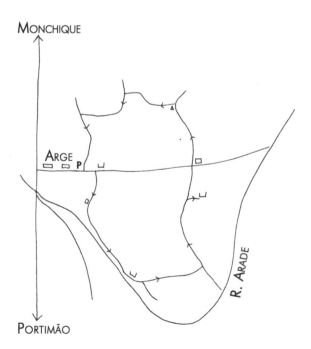

41

As you walk along you will see almond and carob trees on the hillside to your left and the estuary to your right. Soon Estombar and Ferragudo come into view in the distance. Closer by, you will notice olive and oak trees appearing together with dwarf palms. The path is very close to the water's edge and at times it can become submerged, but you will always find a smaller path in amongst the grass. There can be some muddy patches, but don't be put off.

Keep to the water's edge until you come to a ruined farmhouse. Pass behind the house and between the bushes until you come to a fork. Take the left hand one which leads away from the water, passing in front of an old well, before heading gently uphill between rows of carob trees.

On the brow of the hill you will meet a very wide track. Turn left onto it, again gradually climbing upwards. You must stop and look behind where you will see the Portimao and Praia da Rocha skyline and the sea in the distance.

Further along the track make sure you stop again, this time looking to your right where you will see the Rio Arade and Silves in the distance. Immediately in front, you should spot a ruined farmhouse on top of the hill.

Eventually you come to the top of this hill and as the track turns left you will notice a path to your right. About 100m up this path you will find the farmhouse. For the views alone, it is well

worth a short diversion from the main walk. This is also a great place for a short break.

The main track now takes you over the brow of the hill and gently winds downhill. Ignore all other paths until you reach the bottom of the hill and head towards a small white house, which you will see in front of you. The house marks the moment of decision: do you return to your car, or carry on?

The next part of the walk is more strenuous, so if you are not feeling up to it, turn left along the wide unsurfaced red road and in about 15 minutes you will be back at the start of the walk.

If you want to continue, however, cross over this road and pass to the side of the house before taking a left-hand fork which leads uphill. Below to your right you will see a reservoir. The vegetation now changes completely and the path below your feet is very red and sandy. Soon this changes to a more rocky schist as you climb uphill. The climb is short, so just take your time, you will soon reach the top and your exertions will be rewarded with some fine views.

Turn left to pass the trig point. The path becomes stony as it bears right going downhill. When you reach a fork, turn left onto a path that passes around the hillside. You will notice rows of umbrella pine and French lavender. Eventually your path meets a very wide track. Turn left and this will bring you back to the original road and your car.

THE COASTAL PATH

Benagil to Albandeira - 4km.

Walk time: allow a good one and a half hours. In summer there is a beach bar at Albandeira.

Walk grade: fairly easy, although there are one or two relatively steep sections.

To many this is the most picturesque stretch of coast in the whole Algarve. This is real picture postcard stuff: orange and cream cliffs separating beaches of golden sand with wild flowers aplenty along the cliff tops. But all this comes at a price: this area is very popular with visitors who like to walk at least some of the coastal path, so at peak times it can be very busy. Along the path there are several spectacular blowholes. Some are very obvious. Others are hidden by bushes. Take care.

START OF WALK

Benagil is a small fishing village on the coast. To reach it, you turn right at the International School, 3km east of Lagoa on the EN125. Then follow the signs. As you enter the village of Benagil, park at the top of the hill by the restaurant/cafe rather

than turning left to descend steeply to the beach.

THE WALK

Walk down the hill to the first house on the left and go up the steps to the side of it. At the top, go right at the first opportunity and you will soon have wonderful views down to Benagil beach. Now follow the path close to the cliff edge. Soon you will come to a blowhole at the head of a small inlet.

You have to go inland to pass it. Then bear right to follow the cliff edge. The scenery along this section is really quite wonderful and it can take you a long time to make any real progress toward the next beach, which is Marinha. Before reaching Marinha, you must descend to cross a dry valley. There are several alternative paths, all quite stony, so watch your step.

Eventually you will reach the car park above Marinha beach. Turn right and at the far end you will see a stepped path that continues to follow the cliff top. Soon you come to a path off to the right. This leads down to the beach, but the coastal path continues straight on. It climbs slightly and soon you are approaching a large fence around a villa. Take care here because there is another wide blowhole. Continue along the path with the fence on your left. Soon you pass yet another blowhole. Down below there are some really super beaches which appear totally inaccessible except by boat.

Just after the fence, the path heads slightly inland and descends to cross an inlet opposite a small island just off the coast, popular with the local seabirds. Not long after, you have to cross yet another valley and this time you must head further inland to make a relatively easy descent.

The path here is obvious. There are detours off to the cliff edge, which are well worth a visit, and very soon after that you will see a large inlet and the beach of Praia de Albandeira.

You can continue on from here. Again, views are wonderful with more off-shore islands and blowholes, but soon the path will head inland to cross a particularly steep valley. The crossing here is rather tricky, steep and awkward. It is best avoided.

HILLTOPS AND ORANGE GROVES

*A circular walk in the countryside between Silves and
São Bartolomeu de Messines.*

Walk time: allow a good two and a half-hours.

Walk grade: moderate. There are some fairly steep climbs,
but they are very short and the paths are good.

This is a land of fruit trees and vegetable gardens, of small
villages and remote countryside, a land of contrasts. This walk
will show you all that the area has to offer: its beauty, its fertility,
its wildness and its people. It is a chance to appreciate inland
Algarve at its best. An area little touched by the recent
developments that are ever present on the horizon. Enjoy it!

START OF THE WALK

From Silves take the EN124 towards São Bartolomeu de
Messines. After about 12km you will see a turning off to your left
signposted 'Cortes' and 'Torre.' Turn here and drive up to the
village. Park your car on the side of the road, close to a right turn
into the village.

THE WALK

Continue straight along the road and you soon begin to leave
the village. Ignore a road turning off to the right. Instead, follow
the road uphill towards a café. Pass this and several small houses
as you stay on the road.

A wonderful view opens up to your left all the way to the coast.
Soon you can see the mountains of the Serra de Monchique on
your right.

You pass a large orange grove on your left just before you
come to another small hamlet where you pass a row of single-
storey houses on your right. Immediately after the last house in

the row there is a path off to the right that heads downhill (at this point the road you were on begins to climb quite steeply).

As you follow the path down the slope, you pass fig and almond trees on your right before meeting a track coming in from your left. Continue straight down.

Ignore all other turnings. Eventually your path levels out as it follows the contours of the hill. Below to the right are large groves of oranges, lemons and other citrus fruits. When you meet a track that passes up steeply to your left, turn right and follow the track down between orange and lemon trees. The track bends left and then almost immediately right (ignore a turning over a bridge on your left) and meets a surfaced road.

To your left the road forks. Cross over and take the branch that heads downhill. Soon after crossing a bridge, turn right and take the path that heads uphill. Stay to the left when the path forks and climb up to the hilltop where you meet another track. Turn right. You are now walking along the crest of a ridge. There are several steep climbs but they are short. The downhill sections offer some respite and the views as you walk along are fabulous.

Just before probably the steepest climb you will see a large stone on your left. This is believed to be a menhir (an ancient standing stone thought to have been used in fertility rites or linked to the dead). Halfway up the next and final climb there is a waymark on your left. Almost immediately, there is a narrow path off to the left passing through the bushes. Follow this around the hillside and you will meet the track which passes down from the hilltop. Turn left and head downhill until you come to a junction of paths.

Keep straight on, but bear slightly left on a path that passes around the next hillside until you meet another track. Turn left and almost immediately bear right to follow a track that climbs gradually uphill.

This path is deep red and made of clay. For most of the year it

is very hard, but after heavy rains it can be quite muddy and a bit slippery.   Stay on the track, which eventually brings you to the outskirts of the village of Amorosa where you meet a minor road.

Turn right and follow this uphill past some small houses and villas until you meet a broken down wall. Cross the wall and follow a narrow path off to the left that leads downhill and across some abandoned fields. In the distance you can see the rooftop of a new villa. This is where you are heading. It is important to locate yourself here as the farmer has cleared some of the land and in doing so has destroyed the path in parts. Don't worry. Just make for the villa. Pass behind it and meet a wide track. Now you have wonderful views down the valley where you have been walking. On the horizon you can see the modern buildings of Praia da Rocha.

Stay on the track until you come to a junction of paths. Cross straight over and take the narrowest path that leads between fields and heads for the hamlet of Cortes. Once there, your path meets a village street. Follow this between the houses, passing under an arch before turning right into a small square. Turn first left and a road will bring you back to your starting point.

SCENTS OF THE ALGARVE

A circular walk around the Pico Alto escarpment.

Pico Alto dominates the skyline to the east of Messines. There are tremendous views from the high road and path that lead to the trig point at 276 metres. On the way you pass through the tiny village of Pico Alto where time appears to have stood still. Pico Alto is a limestone escarpment and the vegetation here is typical: rosemary, thyme, lavender and cistus are in abundance. In spring, wild flowers, including peonies, orchids, anemones and the large blue scilla, are everywhere. Valleys on either side of the escarpment are filled with rich red soils. They are so fertile that this area has been called the 'garden of the Algarve'. Orange, fig, carob and almond abound together with small fields of salad vegetables. Because the climate here is so mild, many people grow bananas in their garden!

Walk grade: Moderately easy. There is a climb up to the top, but nothing too steep. However, some of the paths are quite rocky and there is also a short but steep downhill section.

Walk time: Allow three hours. This gives you plenty of time at the trig point to admire the views and perhaps have a picnic.

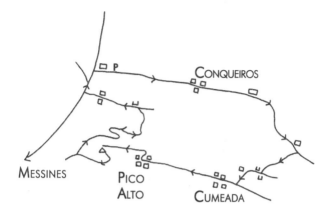

START OF THE WALK

Just before Messines if coming from Alte or Paderne, turn sharp right at the sign for 'Fonte J. Luis'. Continue along the road for about 3km and you come to a small hamlet. Drive through. At the far end the road drops down slightly into a valley before rising quite steeply. In the valley you should see a turning to the right signposted 'Conqueiros'. Turn here. The road is unsurfaced. Park the car somewhere on the roadside.

THE WALK

Continue along the unsurfaced road. Ignore turnings off to the right and left and eventually you come to a small village. Here you walk along a cobbled street between the houses, emerging back onto the unsurfaced road.

Soon you come to a small collection of houses on the left. At this point the road begins to climb gently uphill. About half way up the hillside you pass a farmhouse on the left. At this point you should see a small track on your right which climbs uphill. Take this, and as you take your time getting to the top there are wonderful views overlooking the countryside on your right.

Once at the top of the hill you meet a path. Turn right and pass

51

between some abandoned buildings before passing the side of a house where the path becomes a track that leads to a small, surfaced road. Here you turn right.

This is the tiny village of Cumeada. Eventually, the surfaced road becomes just a track. Continue along it until you come to

another small village. This is Pico Alto. Ignore a turning off to the left continue straight through the village. At the far end is a giant palm tree and, immediately before it, a small house on your right. Turn here to pass along the side of the house. At the back you will see a path that leads off to the left by the side of the garage.

The path here is narrow and passes between dry-stone walls before becoming rather vague. When you come to a fork, go right. You may see a blue dot painted on the bedrock. If not, don't worry; just keep going northwards away from the village. Soon you will reach the edge of the escarpment marked by a dry-stone wall. Turn left here and follow the wall along.

You begin to climb slightly before reaching a cleared field planted with trees. At the far end of the field you can easily cross through the wall onto a path where you turn left. Follow this along until you reach a clearing where you have wonderful views. You can see the trig point ahead of you to your left.

Now follow the narrow path across a small dip before it rises and bears around to the right. The path now passes to the left of some trees before emerging on the right-hand side of the trees and bushes as it heads for the trig point. Once there, the views are spectacular and on a clear day you can see on your left all the way to the coast. In front of you is Messines and the surrounding countryside as you look west towards Silves.

When you decide to leave, walk away from the trig point

keeping to the right. You will soon see a track heading downhill. Follow this. On the steeper parts watch your footing for there are loose stones and rocks around. About halfway down you will see a track off to your left. Turn here and soon you will find yourself walking directly below the trig point. The track follows the hillside for a while before turning left into a field full of almond trees.

Go into the field, turn right, pass through an old wall and follow the edge of the field. Above you to your right there is another field. You should now be following a narrow path that soon becomes a rather wide but vague track where part of the hillside has been cleared so that more trees can be planted.

The track zigzags downhill. After the second turn on a fairly long descent, you should see a narrow path off to the right which follows the hillside.

Take this. Soon you pass a fence on your left. The path then bears left to cross a field before passing to the side of another field and a small orange grove. It drops down onto a track opposite a barn. Turn left and follow the track past some houses before meeting the main road. Turn right and follow the road for a very short time before turning right onto the unsurfaced road where you left your car.

AWAY FROM IT ALL

*A circular walk along the river Algibre
and surrounding countryside.*

Walk time: just over two hours, but you may want to linger and enjoy the solitude.

Walk grade: easy. There is one short, fairly steep descent but the natural lie of the underlying rocks helps by providing 'steps'.

The river Algibre flows from east to west across the central Algarve before meeting the river Quarteira just north of Paderne. The most popular river walk from Paderne is to the very over-rated Paderne castle where only the outer walls remain sufficiently intact to give any indication of its former history. Although 3.5km from the village, the castle is now signposted for those who want to walk there.

This walk begins about 2km east of Paderne and is well off the beaten track. It follows the river for almost an hour before climbing gently up onto the plateau above the river to provide super views. After crossing the plateau and descending back into the valley, orange groves provide the setting for the return to your car. One word of caution: this area is very popular with hunters during the 'open' season, so make sure you do not walk here on Sundays, Thursdays or national holidays.

START OF THE WALK

Turn off the EN395 from Albufeira and drive through the village of Paderne, following the signs for Boliqueime. Just after leaving the village, turn left at the 'Moinho Novo' signpost and follow the road downhill past various villas and houses. After about 2km the road bends sharply right and you will see a small, unsurfaced road almost opposite you. It may or may not be signposted 'Moinho Novo'. Turn here and follow the road past some houses before parking your car.

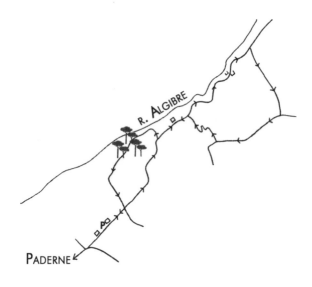

THE WALK

Continue along the road. It soon passes beside a large house and becomes a very straight track. Follow this. Ignore any turnings off to the left and right. The track climbs gently up and then follows the hillside. To your left, down below, are orange groves. Eventually the track drops gently down and you should notice the river on your left as you come to two small buildings. As you pass behind them, the track becomes a narrow path. There is a left fork that leads to the river. You continue straight on. The path now follows the river for about 30 to 40 minutes, depending on your walking speed. You will then come to a small path off to your right. There are no obvious landmarks to help you locate the turning, but just past it a yellow cross has been painted on the bedrock.

The path now climbs gently uphill. It is fairly even, but rocky, and is a complete contrast to the path beside the river. You should notice some dry-stone walls, especially on your right. As you get higher, the countryside becomes more open. The path appears to cross a ruined wall before bearing left to pass over bare land. You are then walking beside, on your left, tiny abandoned fields that have been terraced. There are plenty of olive and almond trees around, but little else.

Eventually you meet a wide track where you turn right. On both sides as you walk along are olive and almond groves and you have good views northwards over the countryside. This is very easy walking. The track appears to end at the edge of a hillside covered in small bushes. To your left there is a path, but back a bit on your right you should see another path that passes between old dry-stone walls. Follow this and soon you come out into a flat field full of olive and almond trees. You are now perched on a small shelf directly above the river.

Turn left and follow an old wall down a slope. After a short distance you will see a path that crosses the wall. Head downhill to your left. There are a lot of small loose stones underfoot, so take care. The path becomes steeper as you descend into the valley. There are several ways down. Choose the best one for you. Once at the bottom you meet a small but clear path. Turn right and follow this and it will bring you back to the riverbank.

Once there, you turn left and follow the path back to the buildings you met near the start of the walk. Here the path becomes a track. Follow this back uphill and, just after bearing left, you should see a track off to your right. Take this. It leads downhill to the edge of an orange grove where you turn left and walk between the trees. At the end of the grove the path bends right, then left, to continue across a large open field. Follow the path. It eventually turns left, then right again, and brings you up to a track. Turn right. You are now on the track you started out on and in about five minutes you should be back at your car.

HEART OF THE ALGARVE

A circular walk through the Barrocal with the opportunity of walking up to the trig point of Rocha dos Soidos (467metres)

Walk time: a comfortable two and a half hours along good paths. Allow an extra 45 minutes if climbing up to the trig point.

Walk grade: moderately easy, although the ascent of Rocha dos Soidos is more strenuous.

This area lies just to the east of the village of Alte, described in guide books as 'one of the prettiest villages' in Portugal. However, in my opinion the village of Benafim, where this walk begins, is in its own way just as pretty and any visitor is spared the crowds, together with numerous cars and jeeps, which fill the streets of Alte in summer. The walk takes you through typical Barrocal scenery and in spring there are plenty of wild flowers. This is a beautiful walk.

START OF THE WALK

From Alte, continue on the main EN124 eastwards towards Salir. After 5kms you come to the village of Benafim. Turn left at the first turning into the village, the 'Rua 11 de Março.' Park your car along this street.

THE WALK

Continue up the street until you come to a smaller street off to your left, the 'Rua da Igreja'. Turn into this and follow it along past the small church. Soon after the church turn right and take a track that leads uphill where you have a wonderful view over the countryside. Descend to a track and turn left. You are now walking through orange and almond groves before passing a farmhouse on your right.

Continue straight on. The path heads downhill. Ignore a turning off to the left. Keep descending and at the bottom turn left to cross a small stream.

Stones have been placed to help you. Once across you soon meet another track. Turn right. Keep straight on until the track almost disappears at the entrance to a large field. You should see a path off to your left. Take this. You climb gently up until you meet another path. Turn left and now you are climbing more steeply uphill. There is a ruined farmhouse on your left. At the top of the hill, stop for a breather and to admire the view.

Ahead is Rocha dos Soidos and to your right, Rocha da Pena.

When you are ready, head downhill. You will meet several paths, but keep straight on; do not bear right across a dry riverbed.

Ignore turnings off to the left until your present track runs into another. Here you turn left to climb uphill. The climb is fairly short and soon you come to a fork marked by several arrows. The writing on each is somewhat faded.

(The right hand path leads up to the trig point of Rocha dos Soidos, a round trip detour of about 40 minutes. If you choose to go to the top, take this path and stay on it ignoring all others. As you near a wall, stay to the right and keep on the small path that climbs to the trig point. Do not be tempted to turn left along a walled-in trail. As you approach the trig point the path passes through a wall, over terraces and back through a wall. The views from the point are spectacular, with Rocha da Pena to the east. Return to the main walk by the same path.)

For the main walk, take the left-hand path and after no more than 100m turn left on a path which heads downhill (be sure not to miss this for it is not as well defined as the path you have been on). You are now winding gently down through olive and oak trees and typical Barrocal limestone scrub.

Eventually you run into a wide track. Turn left. There is a blue arrow painted on the ground rock at this junction. Rocha dos Soidos is now to your left. Continue along this track until it bears left to head downhill.

Turn right. The path is not as obvious as the one you have been following, however some form of heavy machinery has been along the path and cleared everything in it's way. Just follow this cleared land. There may not be a proper path, but the walking is still easy and soon you meet a clear track. Turn left and head downhill.

At the bottom you meet another track. Turn right and soon you come to the junction of paths you met earlier in the walk. Take the one that heads uphill slightly to your right. Follow it up and then down into a wide field. There is an abandoned house to your right. Once in the field turn right and follow the path. Soon you are retracing your steps. When the path forks, bear left to cross over the stream once again and retrace your steps back uphill to Benafim.

A WALK BACK IN TIME

Covões to Portela

Walk time: 1hour 15 minutes or 2 hours
Walk grade: Very easy

This is suitable for all the family, with the option of an uphill climb to give panoramic views and look at the mass of flowers which adorn the hillside in spring.

Covões was almost an abandoned village. Some of the houses have now been lovingly restored, while others remain empty or are just ruins. The village lies at one end of a limestone ridge and the walk along an old medieval donkey track takes us through the abandoned hamlet of Barranquinho to the very small but active hamlet of Portela with its pristine white washed houses.

START OF THE WALK

Covões lies just off the Loulé - Salir road. If coming from Loulé, just before the road descends towards Salir there is a turning to the left, signposted Nave do Barão. Turn here and you will soon see the nameplate 'Covões' and then a road off to the right, which climbs uphill. Turn here and the road will bring you into the village of Covões. There is a small parking space on the right just after you enter the village.

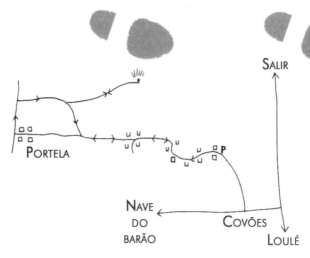

THE WALK

Proceed along the road, which climbs gently uphill. You will notice both abandoned houses and ruined ones as you walk along. Towards the top of the village, several houses have been carefully restored. Dates above the doors indicate that the village was probably thriving at the end of the nineteenth century. At the top of the village, where the road becomes unsurfaced, it passes behind and between houses. Continue along until the track makes a sharp bend to the left. You will notice a smaller track off to your right. This is your path.

The path is straight and runs parallel to the top of the ridge. It passes a number of ruined houses and soon you have wonderful views south to the Espargal ridge. Ignore any turnings off to your left and right; keep on the main path. You will see a wide variety of lime-loving plants as you walk along, including rosemary, winter jasmine, thyme, dwarf palms and, in spring, a wonderful selection of flowers.

When you reach the tiny hamlet of Portela pass between the houses and you will meet a surfaced road. Turn right and soon the road begins to head downhill. Take the first turning on your right, which is a track between dry-stone walls. There are now olive and almond trees either side of the path, which can be a bit stony in parts.

The track bears round to the right and then starts to head uphill. At this point you should notice a path off to your right. (For those who want to stretch their muscles a bit more, or for the flower lovers amongst you, a walk up the hill is well worth while. The views are great and the top makes a super picnic spot. However, to continue the walk you must come down the same way. Do not be tempted to follow any of the other tracks - they will not lead you back to the village.)

Turn right and shortly you will meet the track you walked along towards Portela. Turn left and follow the track back again. Believe me, you will notice many things you missed when you started out. This walk has so much to see in a relatively short distance, it's a delight.

WHAT A CORKER!

A circular walk north of São Bras de Alportel through
rolling countryside dominated by cork oaks.

It is difficult to understand why this area is so overlooked by visitors to the Algarve. Perhaps it is because the main guide books generally ignore it, preferring to write about more glamorous locations. But the setting here is absolutely beautiful - not outstanding - but beautiful in a pastoral way. It fully deserves its reputation of 'nestling between the mountains and the ocean'. This walk takes you through countryside where the cork oak dominates down to the river of Aportel whose fertile banks support a variety of fruit trees and market gardening produce. A gentle but steady climb brings you back to the top and wonderful views south between the hills to the coast.

Walk grade: moderately easy. Most of the paths are very good. There is a climb, but it is steady rather than steep.

Walk time: a comfortable two and a half hours.

START OF THE WALK

Make your way to the centre of São Bras and take the road to Tavira. Turn first left after leaving the central square signposted 'Bico Alto'. Then follow further signs for the village. Bico Alto is about 3km north of São Bras and, although it is well signposted, there are no signs to say you have arrived. It is therefore very easy to drive through and not realise it. However, there is one distinguishing feature: a very large letter box on the left-hand side where you can both post letters and collect them. It is by this box that you should to park your car.

THE WALK

Take the track that leads downhill to the left side of the post box. Ignore a turning off to the left and continue past some houses. The track bends round to the right and then forks. You go right and continue downhill. The path is a bit steep here with loose stones underfoot, but with a little care it should present no problem. At the bottom of the hill continue around to your right and then cross the very small stream to meet another track on the opposite bank. Now turn left and follow the hillside until the path meets another track, which climbs up to the right. Take this track. The climb is steep but short.

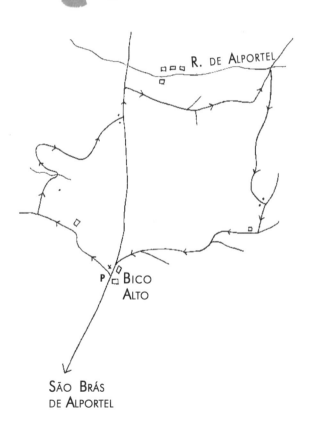

R. DE ALPORTEL

P ⨯ BICO
ALTO

SÃO BRÁS
DE ALPORTEL

At the top, keep on the track. You now have wonderful views over the countryside to the north. Soon you come to an old and rusty gate. It is better to pass it on either side of the gateposts. It brings you to a wide, unsurfaced road. Turn left and head downhill. Again, the views are superb. Eventually you come to a wide turning on your right marked by two signs. Turn here and you will see a number of small white houses to your left down in the valley.

Ignore any turnings off to the left or right. Proceed straight on. The track eventually climbs uphill and then drops down when it becomes more of a narrow path. The path heads gently downhill through the woods and at the bottom it meets a very stony track. This is in fact a dry riverbed.

Turn left and follow it until you reach a wide clearing. In front of you there is the river Alportel. This is a good site for a picnic. As you entered the clearing you should have noticed a wide track to your right that headed uphill away from the river. You need to follow this. As always, take your time and enjoy the countryside. Eventually you will pass through two very smart gateposts. They seem a little incongruous as there are no houses around. Once through, turn right and head back up to the top of the ridge where you will meet a very wide track.

Go right again. You are now following a ridge. You have views to the south towards the coast and to the north over the countryside towards the mountains. Keep straight on. Ignore all turnings. Ahead you should see the houses of Bico Alto in the distance. Eventually you arrive at the edge of the village, passing behind the houses as the track drops down onto the road opposite your car!

WOODLAND WONDERLAND

A circular walk around the countryside of Barranco Velho.

This area to the north of Loulé is a gem. It is an area of hills and valleys where rainfall is heavier than that at the coast, which means there is much more vegetation. Even in the height of summer the hillsides are green, covered mostly with the evergreen cork oak and the ubiquitous cistus. This walk is mostly through woodland, which provides welcome shade from the sun during the summer months. It begins in the village of Barranco Velho where a large church built in the Algarve rustic style in 1944 looks out from the top of the hill. The churchyard has a marvellous viewpoint and from it can be seen endless vistas of hills covered with cork oaks, stretching away to the south. The walk begins by passing through this churchyard. For those who do not feel up to the whole walk, there is an option to finish after the first hour.

Walk grade: moderately easy. The walk is mostly on very good tracks but some of the downhill sections have loose stones underfoot.

Walk time: a comfortable two hours for the whole walk, or one hour and ten minutes for those who wish just to do the first half.

START OF THE WALK

Barranco Velho is 20km north of Loulé. Drive through the village and you come to a main junction where there is a right turning to Alcoutim. Park here. There is a restaurant on your right and a café/ bar on your left.

THE WALK

Almost opposite the restaurant to the right-hand side of the café there is a path that leads uphill past some houses. At the end there is an entrance to the churchyard. Walk in and keep to the left by the wall for panoramic views southwards. At the far end of the wall, turn left through another entrance onto a track that leads through woods. Ignore a turning off to the right. Instead, keep straight on. You should notice some red and yellow markings on the trees. These mark out the whole walk, but you cannot rely on them because local farmers may cut down the trees.

When you come to a junction, bear left. At the next meeting of

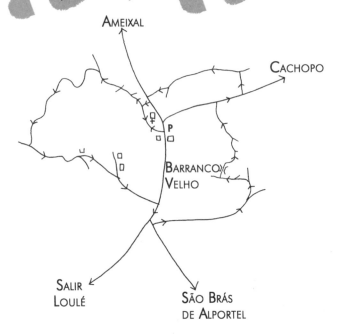

paths, keep straight on. Soon the track forks. Turn left. Not long after the track bends sharply to the right and begins to head downhill. There may be loose stones underfoot, so take care. Eventually you meet another track at which you turn left The track follows the hillside around. When you meet another path, take the left fork which heads uphill towards a ruined house. Soon you pass some very small, terraced fields and houses on your left before meeting a small, surfaced road. Turn right and follow this road until it meets the main road in the centre of the village. If you want to finish the walk now, turn left and follow the road back to your car.

To continue the walk, turn right and follow the road to a large fork. Take the left-hand one and almost immediately turn left at the signpost to 'Javali.' Follow the main track. Ignore any turnings off to left or right.

You eventually find yourself heading downhill and you come to another fork: bear left. Soon after you come to another junction: bear left again. Ignore a turning off to your right: keep straight on. After about five minutes the path begins to head uphill and you should see a small track off to your right. Turn here and you should come almost immediately to a small concrete bridge which you cross and turn right.

You begin to climb gently uphill and come to a turning. Turn left. The path appears quite overgrown in parts and now you have two small but fairly steep climbs before meeting a track. Turn left and, after another short climb, turn left and keep straight on until you meet the main road. There you turn right. After about 200 metres you should see a turning off to the left indicated by a white arrow on the road.

There is a short climb before you turn left and follow the path until you meet a wide track. Turn right and head slightly downhill. Ignore a turning off to your left and soon you come to the main road. Almost opposite you, but slightly to the left, there is a track. Take this and turn almost immediately left. This will bring you back to the churchyard and you can retrace your footsteps back to the car, admiring the view as you go.

RURAL TRADITIONS

A circular walk to the hamlet of Malhada do Peres through the national forest and back along the Zambujosa river valley.

Walk time: Allow two hours fifteen minutes.
Walk grade: Fairly easy along very good tracks and paths.

The countryside north of Tavira feels very remote even though the IP1 is so close by. This walk begins by passing through the 'Mata Nacional', a national forest, although this may be hard to believe because there are so few trees around. The hillsides have been cleared of vegetation and new trees planted. It is not particularly attractive at first, but soon you pass into very picturesque countryside. The hamlet of Malhada do Peres lies in a valley and is well worth a look: the traditional way of life still abounds there. From the hamlet the walk follows the Zambujosa river valley whose fertile soils have been intensively farmed by the local community. It really is beautiful here and there are plenty of good places to picnic.

START OF THE WALK
From Tavira take the EN125 towards Vila Real. After about 3km you pass the large Eurotel on your left. Take the next turning left signposted 'Pensão' and another to the 'Mata Nacional'. About 1km down the road, turn right over a bridge and continue until you come to a junction. Turn left, again at a 'Mata Nacional' sign, and follow the road under the motorway. Keep straight on and you will soon come to a turning to the left to Malhada do Peres. Park here. There is plenty of space by the side of the road.

THE WALK
Walk up the road in the direction of Malhada do Peres. Very soon the road forks: take the left one. Now you are gently climbing uphill along a wide track. As you walk along you will see the new trees planted on the hillsides. They are mostly pines and the ubiquitous eucalyptus.

Soon the track heads downhill to the river and crosses it. As you climb gradually up the other side, the landscape changes. There are now far more trees and also abandoned fields. Once at the top you have a wonderful panorama north over the countryside and you can see the hamlet of Malhada do Peres in the valley below.

Ignore turnings off to the left and right. Continue straight on and down towards the hamlet. When you reach it, turn almost immediately sharp left passing between some houses along a very stony path. You are now heading away from the houses down to a wide, dry riverbed. Cross it going towards the left where you will see a track on the opposite bank. Follow this. On either side of the path there are tiny cultivated fields, each with its own well. Eventually the path heads downhill to another riverbed that must be crossed. As you follow this path the river is crossed several times.

Eventually you will see a small collection of houses up to your right as you cross the riverbed almost diagonally to meet a track. You turn left to cross back over the river and follow the path gently uphill. To your right on the hilltop there are a few houses and you can also see a round building with a thatched roof. This was a house, which is now used to store tools.

Soon you rise up to see the motorway in the distance. Here the path forks. Bear left to pass in front of an old building. The path almost immediately forks again. This time bear right and head downhill to cross yet another riverbed before climbing again. Ignore a turning off to the right. Continue straight on through woodland of umbrella pines. You are now back in the 'Mata Nacional'. This is very easy walking.

After a while you pass a building high up on your left and a large well on your right. The path now heads uphill and you will see a turning off to the left. Turn here and soon you will meet a surfaced road. Turn left and within minutes you will be back at the car.

CASTRO MARIM RESERVE

Walk time: You can complete the walk in a comfortable three hours, the whole circuit being almost 12kms.

Walk grade: moderately easy. Although the reserve is extremely flat, it can be somewhat tiring on the legs if you do the whole walk. The path at the end of the walk is rather overgrown and does require a certain amount of agility, but don't let this put you off.

The Castro Marim nature reserve is a birdwatchers paradise, but even to those who can just about tell a duck from a seagull this is a great place to visit. It may not appear so at first sight. The reserve is flat with few trees and from the car it appears to have very little to offer, but appearances can be deceptive. Here is one of the most important wintering site in Portugal for a wide variety of birds. In spring and autumn the reserve provides a resting-place for many species, particularly waders, as they migrate north or south.

Flamingos can usually be spotted at some point during the walk. White Storks are another attraction; many nest in the olive trees which border the reserve to the north, while others can be seen feeding or resting on the neighbouring marshes. Other commonly seen birds are egrets, spoonbills, black-winged stilts, grey herons and terns.

The main attraction for all these the birds is the abundance of marine organisms upon which they feed in salt pans, which have been used by man since ancient times to produce salt through seawater evaporation.

Because this is a working reserve and the salt pans occupy much of its 2,000 hectares, access is limited. But there is a track which encircles the pans and this provides the basis of our walk.

You must stay on the track. Do not attempt any short cuts across the banks that separate the pans. They are riddled with gaps that are impossible to cross. If your time is limited, then follow the walk for as long as time allows and then return by the same path.

START OF THE WALK

The entrance to the Castro Marim reserve can easily be missed! There are no signs and the only access is by a dirt track off the main road. Drive south from Castro Marim towards Vila Real de Santo Antonio. You soon cross a small river. About 1km on, look for a track off to your right. There is no road sign indicating this turning, but a good marker is a ruined farm building which is found along this track and can be spotted from the road as you approach the turning. Park the car close to this ruin.

If coming from the south, the turning is about 1.5km from the EN125.

THE WALK

Walk down the track away from the road. You will notice the river on your left. To your right there are olive and carob trees. Keep on the main track, which bends right to give you great views of Castro Marim and its castle, before swinging left when it reaches the river. Eventually you some to the saltworks with a gate across the track. This may be locked with a 'no entry' sign. Don't panic. You are on the correct path. These obstacles are to deter wheeled visitors. Just climb the gate and continue.

Now the track winds between the salt pans until it reaches a pumping station. This is the most southerly point of the reserve. Turn left. Now you are walking along the top of a dyke with the river on your right and the railway on the opposite bank.

The path is quite overgrown. Take the line of least resistance, but watch your footing. To your left you will see a really good track running parallel to yours, but do not be tempted to try and cross. It soon swings away. Meeting a much wider and better path rewards your efforts. Now turn right and when you reach another track about 10 minutes later, turn sharp right. This is the track you started out on and will bring you back to your car.

AN OLD FRONTIER

A walk by the Rio Guadiana

Walk time: this 8km walk can be comfortably completed in two hours.

Walk grade: easy on good paths. If there has been a lot of rain, the path by the river may be muddy but still very walkable.

The Rio Guadiana marks the eastern frontier of the Algarve. Flowing gently toward the sea, the river has seen many a bloody battle fought between Spain and Portugal, but today all is quiet and the river provides a wonderful backdrop for this walk.

Most visitors to the Algarve tend to ignore this region, which is a great pity because the tranquility of the countryside has a lot to offer those who take the time and effort to leave the popular resorts. As with many inland areas, the local people have been little affected by the rapid growth along the coastal strip and continue with a way of life that has changed little over the centuries.

START OF THE WALK

The village of Azinhal lies north of the town of Castro Marim
in the eastern Algarve. Leave the IP1 at the junction for Castro
Marim, but turn left on the EN 122 running north to the Alentejo.
Azinhal is about 9 km along this road. On entering the village,
turn right into the village square. Pass through the square, turning
left and then right into a narrow street, which goes towards the
church. Keep on the road passing the church and you will soon
see the cemetery on your right. Here the road becomes unsurfaced,
but there is no problem driving as it is fairly smooth. After about
2km, you will see a trig point on your left. This is a good place to
park the car.

THE WALK

Before you set off, it is well worth going to the trig point to
look at the view and to take stock of the countryside through which
you will be walking. Then continue down the road along which
you were driving and soon you will come to a fork. Turn right.
Stay on this wide track for about 10 minutes before meeting another

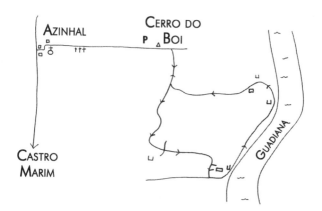

fork. Again take the right fork. The track passes alongside a grove of eucalyptus trees, the only ones you will see on this walk. To your left you may notice bee hives in a distant clearing.

Cistus and oak trees soon replace eucalyptus and after a gentle uphill section you come to another fork. This time branch left. The track now passes gently up and down through rolling countryside with great views of the river and the impressive Guadiana Bridge.

Ignore any tracks off to the left and right: just enjoy the walk. You will notice an abandoned farm to your right and another on the hilltop in front of you. The track passes below this as it heads downhill towards the river.

At the bottom of the hill, turn right. The path follows the bottom of the hill, with the farm high above you on your left. As the river approaches, you meet a track. Turn left and walk around a steep rocky outcrop. (It can be a bit muddy here, as it appears to be a watering spot for animals. If it is too muddy, you can always climb over the rocks.) You will notice an abandoned building on top of the outcrop. This is the old frontier post. You can spot the Spanish version across the river.

The path now follows the bank of the river, with wonderful views upstream. You will immediately notice a change in vegetation, with marsh plants close to the path and cultivated fields to your left. If muddy, you can always walk on the narrow bank to your right. Eventually you come to a landing stage where there may be one or two boats moored. To your left you will see the old customs house. The path now leaves the river's edge and winds gently uphill passing in front of two old farmhouses.

Once again you are in amongst the Cistus and oak trees as you climb upwards with your back to the river. The track now winds back through rolling countryside. Again ignore any tracks off to your left or right, until you meet a wide track coming in from the left. This is the track you originally took. Turn right and very soon you will be back at the trig point. Turn left towards the trig point and your car.